Journal Your Way to HOPE

Find Strength When You Have Lost All Hope

MATT PAVLIK

BRINGING YOUR
POTENTIAL
TO LIGHT

Christian Concepts
Centerville, Ohio

Journal Your Way To Hope
Copyright © 2020 by Matt Pavlik.

All rights reserved. No part of this book may be used or reproduced in any manner whatsoever without written permission except in the case of brief quotations embodied in critical articles or reviews.

Published in the United States of America by Christian Concepts (christianconcepts.com), an imprint of New Reflections Counseling, Inc. (newreflectionscounseling.com).

Although the author is a professional counselor, this book is not intended to be a replacement for professional counseling.

First Edition: April 2020

REL012150 RELIGION / Christian Living / Devotional Journal

Pavlik, Matthew Edward, 1971-
Journal Your Way To Hope / Matt Pavlik.

ISBN: 978-1-951866-01-3 (softcover)

1. Spiritual journals—Authorship—Religious aspects—Christianity
2. Diaries—Authorship—Religious aspects—Christianity

Journaling, Hope, Healing, Growth, Self-acceptance, Meaning (Philosophy), Rejection (Psychology), Self-deception

Scripture quotations marked NLT are taken from the Holy Bible, New Living Translation, copyright © 1996, 2004, 2015 by Tyndale House Foundation. Used by permission of Tyndale House Publishers, Inc., Carol Stream, Illinois 60188. All rights reserved.

Scripture quotations marked (NIV) are taken from the Holy Bible, New International Version®, NIV®. Copyright © 1973, 1978, 1984, 2011 by Biblica, Inc.™ Used by permission of Zondervan. All rights reserved worldwide. www.zondervan.comThe "NIV" and "New International Version" are trademarks registered in the United States Patent and Trademark Office by Biblica, Inc.™

Scripture quotations marked ESV are from the ESV® Bible (The Holy Bible, English Standard Version®), copyright © 2001 by Crossway Bibles, a publishing ministry of Good News Publishers. Used by permission. All rights reserved.

Scripture quotations marked TPT are from The Passion Translation®. Copyright © 2017, 2018 by Passion & Fire Ministries, Inc. Used by permission. All rights reserved. ThePassionTranslation.com.

Amplified Bible (AMP) Copyright © 1954, 1958, 1962, 1964, 1965, 1987 by The Lockman Foundation, La Habra, CA. All rights reserved. Used by Permission.

Scripture quotations marked (CEV) are from the Contemporary English Version Copyright © 1991, 1992, 1995 by American Bible Society, Used by Permission.

IMAGES

Truth #01: freepik - Omelapics: 1190949
Truth #02: pixabay - EvgeniT: 2611199
Truth #03: pixabay - tung256: 2545754
Truth #04: pixabay - Larisa-K: 219972
Truth #05: pixabay - pixel2013: 3156176
Truth #06: pixabay - ZIPNON: 1690608
Truth #07: pixabay - mskathrynne: 3674785
Truth #08: pixabay - Free-Photos: 801742
Truth #09: pixabay - Johannes Plenio: 4257726
Truth #10: pixabay - Evgeni Tcherkasski: 4451281
Truth #11: pixabay - ColdSmiling: 789501
Truth #12: pixabay - aatlas: 299018
Truth #13: pixabay - 8013345: 3324569
Truth #14: pixabay - tpsdave: 1950873
Truth #15: unsplash - Logan Armstrong: sand
Truth #16: pixabay - PublicDomainPictures: 70908, mohamed Hassan:3494652
Truth #17: pxHere - 102334
Truth #18: pixabay - Free-Photos: 336693
Truth #19: pixabay - Dan Williams: 3122660
Truth #20: pixabay - Gerd Altmann: 4433376
Truth #21: pixabay - Free-Photos: 947331
Truth #22: pixabay - _Marion: 279862, mtajmr: 1906550, Marisa04: 3051422
Truth #23: pixabay - tpsdave: 2608985
Truth #24: pixabay - tpsdave: 1748642
Truth #25: pixabay - PIRO4D: 2534484, Gellinger: 3065387
Truth #26: pixabay - Barbara Jackson: 571715
Truth #27: pixabay - jplenio: 3215625
Truth #28: adobe - 218368808
Truth #29: pixabay - KELLEPICS: 2546204
Truth #30: pixabay - sasint: 1822503, 1822702

CONTENTS

Introduction: What Good is Hope? 1
Truth #01: Light Always Overcomes Darkness 4
Truth #02: Light Floods Your Heart With Confident Hope 8
Truth #03: Christ's Love for You is Relentless 12
Truth #04: God Rescues You During Times of Adversity 16
Truth #05: God is an Endless Supply of Mercy 20
Truth #06: God is Committed to You Throughout Your Lifetime 24
Truth #07: God Promises You Will Inherit Eternal Life 28
Truth #08: Nothing is Impossible for God 32
Truth #09: God Supplies the Faith You Need 36
Truth #10: God Comforts You When You Doubt 40
Truth #11: When You Hope in the Future, You Receive Hope Today 44
Truth #12: God Notices When You Put Your Hope in Him 48
Truth #13: God is Trustworthy Even When It Seems Like He Isn't 52
Truth #14: God Can Be Trusted To Keep His Promises 56
Truth #15: Belief Activates God's Power in Your Life 60
Truth #16: Seeking God Activates His Plans 64
Truth #17: God is On Your Side, Ready to Help 68
Truth #18: God is With You Wherever You Go 72
Truth #19: Your Suffering Assures You of Your Salvation 76
Truth #20: God's Plans for Your Good Outlast Your Suffering 80
Truth #21: You Share in Suffering So You Can Share in Glory 84
Truth #22: Your Suffering and Hard Work Are Not in Vain 88
Truth #23: God Satisfies Your Soul 92
Truth #24: God Fills You With Joy, Peace, and Hope 96
Truth #25: God is an Endless Supply of Strength 100
Truth #26: Confident Hope Leads to Bold Action 104
Truth #27: God's Will is That You Become Complete 108
Truth #28: God Strengthens You to Endure All Things 112
Truth #29: God Doesn't Want You To Give Up or Lose Hope 116
Truth #30: When God Gave You Life, He Gave You Dreams 120

What Good is Hope?

With hope you can endure anything. Without hope everything is a burden. Hope lifts your spirit like helium lifts a balloon. Hope also pads your soul, absorbing the shock of life's journey down a bumpy road.

Whenever life disappoints, hope has a genuinely encouraging response. You can lose your job, your car, your house, your health, and even a loved one, but no one can take away from you God's gift of eternal life.

Don't put your hope in anything you can lose. This kind of worldly hope leads to despair and doubt. To benefit from hope, you must put your hope only in what you can't lose.

*He is no fool who gives what he cannot keep
to gain what he cannot lose.*
—Jim Elliot

How about you? What kind of hope do you have? Are you so discouraged you've given up hope?

Life beats you down. Darkness engulfs you. Your brokenness is all you can see. Then you doubt God's goodness. Standing up and walking confidently forward can seem impossible. God's truth can seem irrelevant or even useless.

To doubt God's truth is to give in to despair. Despair has physical (position) and mental (attitude) components. Do the following sound like you?
- Position: dead end, trapped, confined, held back, no traction, sinking in quicksand, no way out, frozen.
- Attitude: defeated, fatalistic, doomed, failed before started, negative, impossible, pessimistic.

When you feel hopeless, you are deceived. When God is involved, there is always hope. The truth of the Gospel renders despair an illusion. Hope is real when what you hope in is real. Hope is full assurance that outrageously better times are on their way.

When God is involved, a lot is possible. Is there hope for you? Yes, there is, even if you are discouraged and full of doubt. Whenever all you see is a dead-end, there is always a hidden door that leads forward.

> *The LORD is there to rescue*
> *all who are discouraged and have given up hope.*
> —Psalm 34:18 CEV

God is on your side, actively working to lift you out of despair. As you move away from despair, you experience a cautious but growing optimism. You start to believe there is a way out. Hopeless becomes maybe. Impossible becomes I'll give it a try. You're no longer frozen, but warming up.

Journal Your Way To Hope

What does experiencing a complete and pure hope look like? When you're hopeful, you're confident of the way forward even when you can't fully see it. You're joyful, energetic, motivated, certain, assured, sold-out, all-in. You're not just warm or hot; you're on fire.

Now to him who is able to do far more abundantly than all that we ask or think, according to the power at work within us, to him be glory in the church and in Christ Jesus throughout all generations, forever and ever. Amen.
—Ephesians 3:20-21 ESV

How To Use This Book

You'll gain more from your journaling experience when you journal in layers. Journaling in layers has four steps:
1. **Represent**: communicate what is internal or subconscious by expressing it in some external or explicit medium (words, symbols, sculptures).
2. **Rest**: acknowledge what you expressed, then wait. Let it simmer, percolate, steep. Focus on something else.
3. **Review**: revisit what you expressed, taking it back in and looking for understanding and meaning.
4. **Repeat**: return to step 1.

This book has 30 truth lessons. Respond to each truth, then return at a regular interval (1 day, 1 week, or 1 month) to reflect on the truth again, including all of your previous responses. Then, write a new response. This will deepen the truth for you.

If you want more details about this method, grab a free copy of *Journal In Layers So You Can Soar Like Eagles* at ChristianConcepts.com. It's a short read and it will help you gain more from your journaling.

Light Always Overcomes Darkness

In him was life, and that life was the light of all mankind. The light shines in the darkness, and the darkness has not overcome it.

—John 1:4-5 NIV

...the people dwelling in darkness
have seen a great light,
and for those dwelling
in the region and shadow of death,
on them a light has dawned.

—Matthew 4:16 ESV

MATT PAVLIK

Even in the inevitable moments when all seems hopeless, men know that without hope they cannot really live, and in agonizing desperation they cry for the bread of hope.
—Martin Luther King, Jr.

Jesus replied, "I am the bread of life. Whoever comes to me will never be hungry again. Whoever believes in me will never be thirsty.
—John 6:35 NLT

Journal Your Way to Hope

Because of Jesus, a bad day is never the end of your story. The night is dark, but a new day will dawn.

No matter how hard darkness presses on your life, it can't stop the light from shining. Darkness can't make light flee because darkness is only the absence of light. No matter how hopeless you've become, bread is available to nourish your hope. Even in your darkest moments, you can feel hopeful by remembering that Jesus is the light-life.

How hopeless do you feel? What darkness looms? What cloud of doom hangs? How hopeful do you feel? What light is shining through the darkness, even if only a sliver? Your situation may feel hopeless, but a great light is shining. Ask Jesus to shine His light on you so you can abound in all hope.

Truth #02

Light Floods Your Heart With Confident Hope

I pray that your hearts will be flooded with light so that you can understand the confident hope he has given to those he called, and the rich and glorious inheritance he has given to his holy people.

—Ephesians 1:18 NLT

All praise to God, the Father of our Lord Jesus Christ, who has blessed us with every spiritual blessing in the heavenly realms because we are united with Christ. Even before he made the world, God loved us and chose us in Christ to be holy and without fault in his eyes.

—Ephesian 1:3-4 NLT

MATT PAVLIK

If the child of God begins to doubt his acceptance before God, he will have no heart [no hope, no desire, no motivation] to be holy and will sink into disobedience, discouragement and sin.

—A. B. Simpson.

Therefore, there is now no condemnation for those who are in Christ Jesus, because through Christ Jesus the law of the Spirit who gives life has set you free from the law of sin and death.

—Romans 8:1-2 NIV

Journal Your Way to Hope

God provides light as a spiritual blessing, a healing power. Your attitude toward God depends on your understanding of God's acceptance. When you focus on negative circumstances, your confidence in God wavers. As soon as you refocus on God, you draw strength. When you consider God's goodness, what attribute empowers you to face your daily challenges?

You have God's unconditional, abundant favor—primarily spiritually, secondarily physically. You have permanent peace with God.

God's truth shines in your heart. How much of it have you been able to receive? Your inheritance is coming. Until then will you allow the light to flood your heart? Will you accept God's acceptance?

Christ's Love for You is Relentless

Can anything ever separate us from Christ's love? Does it mean he no longer loves us if we have trouble or calamity, or are persecuted, or hungry, or destitute, or in danger, or threatened with death? (As the Scriptures say, "For your sake we are killed every day; we are being slaughtered like sheep.") No, despite all these things, overwhelming victory is ours through Christ, who loved us. And I am convinced that nothing can ever separate us from God's love. Neither death nor life, neither angels nor demons, neither our fears for today nor our worries about tomorrow—not even the powers of hell can separate us from God's love. No power in the sky above or in the earth below—indeed, nothing in all creation will ever be able to separate us from the love of God that is revealed in Christ Jesus our Lord.

—Romans 8:35-39 NLT

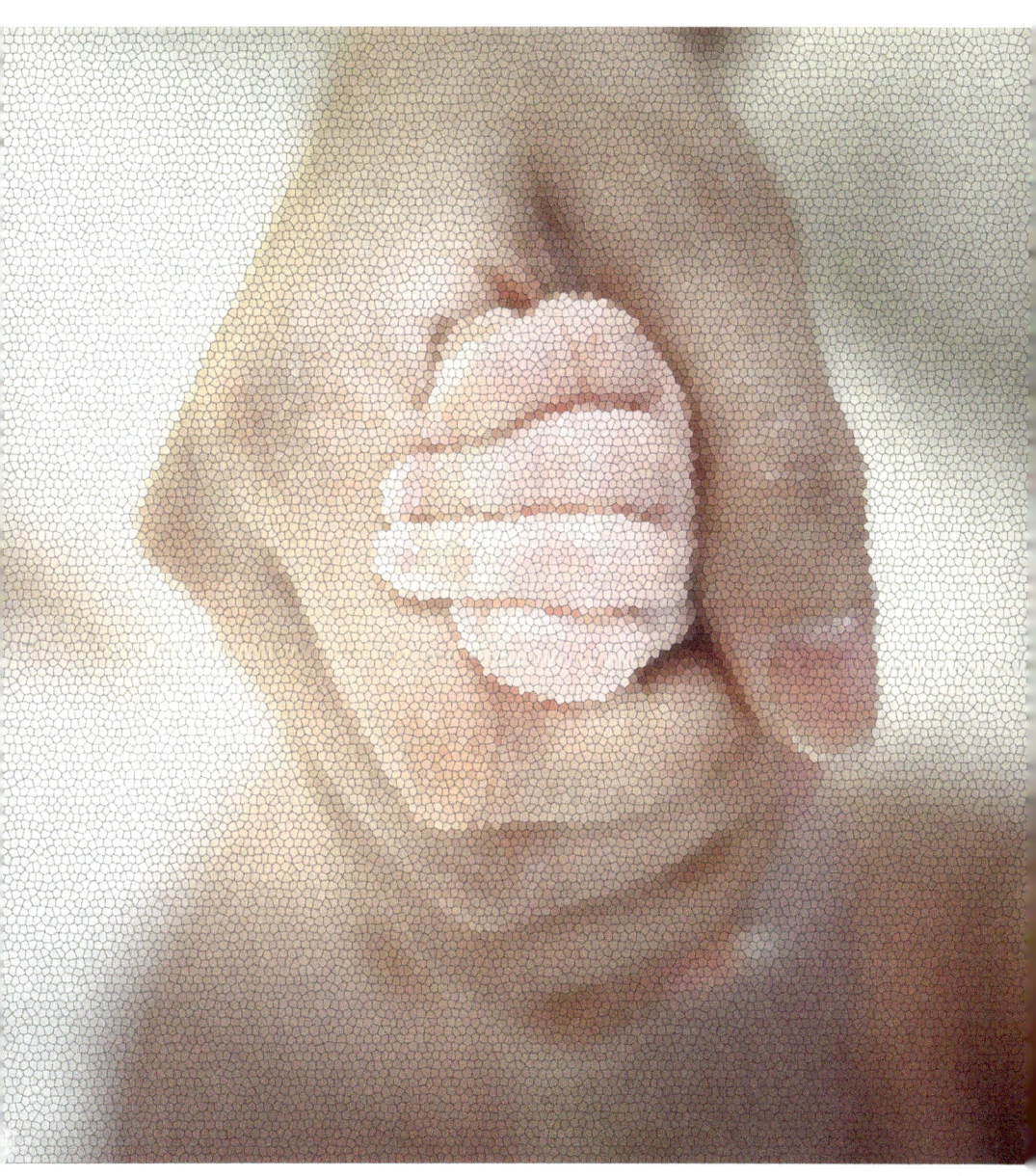

MATT PAVLIK

No matter how bad you mess up, God loves you, and there's nothing you can do about it.

—Lecrae

God is love. Love is patient and kind; love does not envy or boast; it is not arrogant or rude. It does not insist on its own way; it is not irritable or resentful; it does not rejoice at wrongdoing, but rejoices with the truth. Love bears all things, believes all things, hopes all things, endures all things.

—1 John 4:8, 1 Corinthians 13:4-7 ESV

Journal Your Way to Hope

Do you ever feel like you are slipping into darkness or hopelessness? Once you become a Christian, God's hand grasps your hand and nothing can sever the connection, regardless of how you feel. If nothing can separate you from God's love, nothing can separate you from hope.

Don't give up. There is no reason to give up. God is on your side and is fighting for your victory. You are permanently exempt from condemnation. He made you for a purpose. When you stop trying, your purpose is delayed.

There's always hope. You can mess up all day and seem to exhaust God's patience, but His patience has no end. God is always full of never-ceasing love.

What stands in the way of you realizing Christ's love?

Truth #04

God Rescues You During Times of Adversity

But blessed are those who trust in the LORD and have made the LORD their hope and confidence. They are like trees planted along a riverbank, with roots that reach deep into the water. Such trees are not bothered by the heat or worried by long months of drought. Their leaves stay green, and they never stop producing fruit.
—Jeremiah 17:7-8 NLT

*The Lord hears his people when they call to him for help.
He rescues them from all their troubles.
The Lord is close to the brokenhearted;
he rescues those whose spirits are crushed.
The righteous person faces many troubles,
but the Lord comes to the rescue each time.*
—Psalm 34:17-19 NLT

MATT PAVLIK

An infinite God can give all of Himself to each of His children. He does not distribute Himself that each may have a part, but to each one He gives all of Himself as fully as if there were no others.

—A. W. Tozer

I waited patiently for the Lord to help me, and he turned to me and heard my cry. He lifted me out of the pit of despair, out of the mud and the mire. He set my feet on solid ground and steadied me as I walked along. He has given me a new song to sing, a hymn of praise to our God.

—Psalm 40:1-3 NLT

Journal Your Way to Hope

Seeing God as your ally and protector, aligning yourself with Him, and being on His team all open a connection with Him that shields you from psychological and spiritual harms such as irritation, worry, doubt, fear, and weakness.

God sustains you during drought and distress. God's delay isn't because He lacks power, speed, or time. He isn't too busy to notice you. You don't have to stand in line waiting for others to finish their time with God. You can boldly approach God at any time (Hebrews 4:16).

You might be crushed, brokenhearted, or in despair without any option but to wait for God's rescue. The waiting can take very different courses. You can wait patiently and peacefully or you can wait anxiously, bitterly, and bothered.

Truth #05

God is an Endless Supply of Mercy

*"O LORD," I prayed, "have mercy on me.
Heal me, for I have sinned against you."*
—Psalm 41:4 NLT

The steadfast love of the LORD never ceases; his mercies never come to an end; they are new every morning; great is your faithfulness.
—Lamentations 3:22–23 ESV

MATT PAVLIK

*The very contradictions in my life
are in some ways signs of God's mercy to me.*
—Thomas Merton

*How satisfied you are when you demonstrate tender mercy!
For tender mercy will be demonstrated to you.*
—Matthew 5:7 TPT

Journal Your Way to Hope

You notice other's faults because they cause you pain. You avoid seeing your faults because that is also uncomfortable. Do you find it easier to forgive the person who sins against you, or yourself when you sin?

Have you ever been caught being hypocritical? Perhaps you gladly receive forgiveness but struggle to offer it for the same failings. The enemy wants you to feel condemned. Thankfully, God is merciful concerning your internal inconsistencies.

God saves you from the hopelessness of unforgiveness. In your struggle to forgive yourself, let God's kindness have the final word. If the God of the universe proclaims you are forgiven, then the matter is settled. No matter how bad you mess up, God can make it better. Thank God for His mercy.

Truth #06

God is Committed to You Throughout Your Lifetime

*I will be your God throughout your lifetime—
until your hair is white with age.
I made you, and I will care for you.
I will carry you along and save you.*

—Isaiah 46:4 NLT

It is the Lord who goes before you. He will be with you; he will not leave you or forsake you. Do not fear or be dismayed.

—Deuteronomy 31:8 ESV

MATT PAVLIK

Let God's promises shine on your problems.
—Corrie Ten Boom

And because of his glory and excellence, he has given us great and precious promises. These are the promises that enable you to share his divine nature and escape the world's corruption caused by human desires.
—2 Peter 1:4 NLT

Journal Your Way to Hope

God keeps all of His promises. God's commitment to you is forever; His love is eternal. Look to God's promises when you encounter problems. Allow Him to carry you and save you. Those who leave everything in God's hand will see God's hand in everything.

God enables you to endure the harshness of this life by giving you His divine nature. Whatever happens, don't doubt God. What you want is important, but knowing God and His intentions for all of life is more important.

God accepts responsibility for you. He's your Father; you're His child. You will have difficulty and hardship, but God is with you and He will see you through it all. What is God promising you? Where have you seen His commitment to you?

God Promises You Will Inherit Eternal Life

Truly, truly, I say to you, whoever hears my word and believes him who sent me has eternal life. He does not come into judgment, but has passed from death to life.

—John 5:24 ESV

This letter is from Paul, a slave of God and an apostle of Jesus Christ. I have been sent to proclaim faith to those God has chosen and to teach them to know the truth that shows them how to live godly lives. This truth gives them confidence that they have eternal life, which God—who does not lie—promised them before the world began.

Because of his grace he made us right in his sight and gave us confidence that we will inherit eternal life.

—Titus 1:1-2, 3:7 NLT

MATT PAVLIK

Totally without hope one cannot live. To live without hope is to cease to live. Hell is hopelessness. It is no accident that above the entrance to Dante's hell is the inscription: "Leave behind all hope, you who enter here."
—Fyodor Dostoevsky

My sheep hear my voice, and I know them, and they follow me. I give them eternal life, and they will never perish, and no one will snatch them out of my hand.
—John 10:27-28 ESV

Journal Your Way to Hope

God promises you eternal life, not temporary life. He wants you to be sure you have it. After you've passed from death to life, you're under the Great Shepherd's care. Jesus will not allow even one of His sheep to become lost beyond His reach. God permanently seals the doorway to death for you.

Saving faith comes by hearing the Gospel message and believing it. Real hope is based on the guarantee of future events—the ultimate one being your inheritance of eternal life.

Hope must have an immovable anchor in God and His promises. God is trustworthy. He doesn't go back on His word. He doesn't take back His gifts. Where is your hope anchored? How confident are you that God has secured eternal life for you?

Nothing is Impossible for God

For nothing will be impossible with God.
—Luke 1:37 ESV

'Ah, Lord GOD! It is you who have made the heavens and the earth by your great power and by your outstretched arm! Nothing is too hard for you.
—Jeremiah 32:17 ESV

MATT PAVLIK

"My hope is based on a God who can do and will do the impossible. My hope is based on a God who has defeated death itself. We can't live without hope. When we keep hoping, we keep living."
—Pete Wilson, Let Hope in

Then, when our dying bodies have been transformed into bodies that will never die, this Scripture will be fulfilled: "Death is swallowed up in victory. O death, where is your victory? O death, where is your sting?" For sin is the sting that results in death, and the law gives sin its power. But thank God! He gives us victory over sin and death through our Lord Jesus Christ.
—1 Corinthians 15:54-57 NLT

Journal Your Way to Hope

God caused a virgin to be with child and give birth. He defeated death. He can accomplish anything. God limited Jesus to enter history at just the right time (Galatians 4:4-5).

God has a plan for your life which involves His perfect timing for what He wants to accomplish in your life. God can flip a switch at any moment. When the time is right, God will move mountains to resolve your problems and unleash His purposes for your life.

How patient are you as you wait on God? Sometimes God has us wait days, sometimes years, and sometimes for life. No matter how long you must wait, God's power remains the same. His potential is unlimited. Whatever you're going through is meaningful because you are important to God.

Truth #09

God Supplies the Faith You Need

For by grace you have been saved through faith. And this is not your own doing; it is the gift of God, not a result of works, so that no one may boast. For we are God's masterpiece. He has created us anew in Christ Jesus, so we can do the good things he planned for us long ago.

—Ephesians 2:8-10 NLT

So faith comes from hearing, and hearing through the word of Christ.

—Romans 10:17 ESV

MATT PAVLIK

*Faith is to believe what you do not see;
the reward of this faith is to see what you believe.*
—Saint Augustine

And let us run with endurance the race God has set before us. We do this by keeping our eyes on Jesus, the champion who initiates and perfects our faith.
—Hebrews 12:1-2 NLT

Journal Your Way to Hope

God is your source, your everything, your all. When God asks you to do something, He provides the means for you to be successful. Grace and faith are God's gifts to you so you are able to hear God, trust Him, and act on His direction. Faith grants you power to see with spiritual eyes. By faith you see that what you hope for is real. You see it clearly enough to act.

The devil's lies are always false, no matter how true they seem to you. When you believe the lies, you double your misery. First is the negative experience. Second is believing your situation is hopeless.

God's truth is always true, no matter what happens to you. You've been saved and predestined for good works. Ask God for more faith. What can you see with your spiritual eyes?

God Comforts You When You Doubt

*When doubts filled my mind,
your comfort gave me renewed hope and cheer.*
—Psalm 94:19 NLT

Praise be to the God and Father of our Lord Jesus Christ, the Father of compassion and the God of all comfort, who comforts us in all our troubles, so that we can comfort those in any trouble with the comfort we ourselves receive from God. For just as we share abundantly in the sufferings of Christ, so also our comfort abounds through Christ.
—2 Corinthians 1:3-5 NIV

MATT PAVLIK

Doubt is most often the source of our powerlessness. To doubt is to be faithless, to be without hope or belief. When we doubt, our self-talk sounds like this: 'I don't think I can. I don't think I will.'... To doubt is to have faith in the worst possible outcome. It is to believe that even if I do well, something I don't know about will get in the way, sabotage me, or get me in the end.
—Blaine Lee Pardoe

And without faith it is impossible to please God, because anyone who comes to him must believe that he exists and that he rewards those who earnestly seek him.
—Hebrews 11:6 NIV

Journal Your Way to Hope

Times of suffering and doubt will come. When you worry you are expressing mistrust in God. A negative image of God can prevent you from receiving comfort. Open yourself to fully believe that He exists and He wants to comfort you.

God is the Father of mercies and God of all comfort. He meets sin with grace and doubt with comfort. God forgave all your sins—past, present, and future (Colossians 2:14). Rejoice in your freedom. Your future is secured. Your past is forgiven. Your present can overflow with hope.

The secret to feeling hopeful is to ask God to reveal His kingdom (Matthew 6:33). When you suffer for being a Christian, God promises you will be comforted by seeing His spiritual reality. Risk asking God to reveal His kingdom to you.

When You Hope in the Future, You Receive Hope Today

Even when there was no reason for hope, Abraham kept hoping—believing that he would become the father of many nations. For God had said to him, "That's how many descendants you will have!"
—Romans 4:18 NLT

We were given this hope when we were saved. If we already have something, we don't need to hope for it. But if we look forward to something we don't yet have, we must wait patiently and confidently.
—Romans 8:24-25 NLT

MATT PAVLIK

The trust that allows us to embrace uncertainty has three aspects: belief in the provision of God, belief in the promises of God, and belief in the power of God.
—Pete Wilson, What Keeps You Up at Night?

And we believers also groan, even though we have the Holy Spirit within us as a foretaste of future glory, for we long for our bodies to be released from sin and suffering. We, too, wait with eager hope for the day when God will give us our full rights as his adopted children, including the new bodies he has promised us.
—Romans 8:23 NLT

Journal Your Way to Hope

God wants you to keep hoping in His promises even when hoping makes no sense to you. When God told Abraham to sacrifice Isaac, Abraham couldn't rely on logic. Obeying God meant trusting Him and attempting an irrational action.

Eagerly hoping for your perfect body lightens the burden you carry today. As you are filled with hope you become filled with patience and confidence. While you're waiting, you have the Holy Spirit as a foretaste of future glory.

When you look at life with your own understanding you can end up experiencing debilitating uncertainty. But when you borrow God's understanding by trusting Him, you'll experience hopeful assurance. What small step can you take today because of God's future fulfillment of His promise?

Truth #12

God Notices
When You Put Your Hope in Him

*The eyes of the Lord are upon
even the weakest worshipers who love him—
those who wait in hope and expectation
for the strong, steady love of God.
God will deliver them from death,
even the certain death of famine,
with no one to help.
The Lord alone is our radiant hope
and we trust in him with all our hearts.
His wrap-around presence will strengthen us.*

—Psalm 33:18-21 TPT

MATT PAVLIK

Pray, and let God worry.
—Martin Luther

God cares for you, so turn all your worries over to him.
—1 Peter 5:7 CEV

Journal Your Way to Hope

God doesn't worry like people worry. God is capable of meeting all deficiencies with abundant power. When people worry, they worry from a place of spiritual poverty and powerlessness. Worriers are secretly desperate for power and control.

You can't manufacture your own power, but you can accept God's power. He is strong enough to "worry" for all of creation. Jesus shouldered the weight of all weakness while on the cross.

Shift your burdens to God, and immediately new energy will surge within you. Hope in nothing but the Lord. Trust your whole heart only to the Lord. What are you worried about? What keeps you up a night? What heavy burdens are you ready to release into God's care?

Truth #13

God is Trustworthy Even When It Seems Like He Isn't

*Even though the fig trees have no blossoms,
and there are no grapes on the vines;
even though the olive crop fails,
and the fields lie empty and barren;
even though the flocks die in the fields,
and the cattle barns are empty,
yet I will rejoice in the LORD!
I will be joyful in the God of my salvation!
The Sovereign LORD is my strength!
He makes me as surefooted as a deer,
able to tread upon the heights.*

—Habakkuk 3:17-19 NLT

*Be patient and trust the Lord.
Don't let it bother you
when all goes well for those
who do sinful things.*

—Psalm 37:7 CEV

MATT PAVLIK

The theological virtue of hope is the patient and trustful willingness to live without closure, without resolution, and still be content and even happy because our Satisfaction is now at another level, and our Source is beyond ourselves.
—Richard Rohr

We are never defeated unless we give up on God.
—Ronald Reagan

Though he slay me, I will hope in him.
—Job 13:15 ESV

Journal Your Way to Hope

Though evidence might seem to point to God's betrayal, you are still better off trusting God than trusting yourself. Paul found the secret of being content in all circumstances and you can, too (Philippians 4:11-12). When you suffer, one of the significant choices you have is to accept God as either good or evil. Will you move toward Him or away from Him?

For hope to thrive, heaven must become a greater reality than all your circumstances. The more difficulties you've faced early in life, the harder it will be to see the positive reality of heaven. But the greater contrast creates a greater appreciation for heaven. God doesn't torture any of His children. After you move beyond your anger for life's difficulties and trust God, heaven becomes an amazing source of encouragement.

Truth #14

God Can Be Trusted To Keep His Promises

So God has given both his promise and his oath. These two things are unchangeable because it is impossible for God to lie. Therefore, we who have fled to him for refuge can have great confidence as we hold to the hope that lies before us. This hope is a strong and trustworthy anchor for our souls. It leads us through the curtain into God's inner sanctuary. Jesus has already gone in there for us. He has become our eternal High Priest in the order of Melchizedek.

—Hebrews 6:18-20 NLT

MATT PAVLIK

*Never be afraid to trust
an unknown future to a known God.*
—Corrie Ten Boom

*Let us hold tightly without wavering to the hope we affirm,
for God can be trusted to keep his promise.*
—Hebrews 10:23 NLT

Journal Your Way to Hope

God's character is unchangeable; He doesn't lie. God's oaths are unchangeable. God doesn't change His mind about His promises. Jesus has gone ahead of us to secure God's promises. He is your Forever Priest, always interceding on your behalf. You won't be found embarrassed for hoping in God. He wants you to have full assurance of your hope (Hebrews 6:11, 7:24-25).

Can you see how much effort God has taken to win your trust? God is worthy of your trust. If God can't be trusted, then who can? Hopelessness is having no one to trust.

As a believer, you can learn who God really is. To know God is to have eternal life (John 17:3). How does it feel to know that God keeps His promises?

Belief Activates God's Power in Your Life

"How long has this been happening?" Jesus asked the boy's father. He replied, "Since he was a little boy. The spirit often throws him into the fire or into water, trying to kill him. Have mercy on us and help us, if you can." "What do you mean, 'If I can'?" Jesus asked. "Anything is possible if a person believes." The father instantly cried out, "I do believe, but help me overcome my unbelief!"
—Mark 9:21-24 NLT

For God is working in you, giving you the desire and the power to do what pleases him.
—Philippians 2:13 NLT

MATT PAVLIK

You never know how much you really believe anything until its truth or falsehood becomes a matter of life and death to you. It is easy to say you believe a rope to be strong and sound as long as you are merely using it to cord a box. But suppose you had to hang by that rope over a precipice. Wouldn't you then first discover how much you really trusted it?
—C.S. Lewis, A Grief Observed

Jesus told them, "This is the only work God wants from you: Believe in the one he has sent."
—John 6:29 NLT

Journal Your Way to Hope

Like the father of the boy in Mark 9, we are a mixture of belief and unbelief. Your work is to believe, but Jesus will even help you with your unbelief.

When God asks you to believe, He wants you to develop confidence beyond all doubt. He wants you to be sure you're focused on what God is doing, just like Jesus did (John 5:19). When you ask God for wisdom and other good gifts, He wants you to be fully aware of, and fully believe in, exactly who you're asking (James 1:5-6).

Belief is the foundation of all good works. Jesus invites you to participate in His ministry. Do you believe Jesus can do it (the it is whatever you need to trust him for)? Activate God's power by telling Him what you believe.

Truth #16

Seeking God Activates His Plans

Keep on asking, and you will receive what you ask for. Keep on seeking, and you will find. Keep on knocking, and the door will be opened to you. For everyone who asks, receives. Everyone who seeks, finds. And to everyone who knocks, the door will be opened. You parents—if your children ask for a loaf of bread, do you give them a stone instead? Or if they ask for a fish, do you give them a snake? Of course not! So if you sinful people know how to give good gifts to your children, how much more will your heavenly Father give good gifts to those who ask him.

—Matthew 7:7-11 NLT

MATT PAVLIK

When we lose one blessing, another is often most unexpectedly given in its place.
—C.S. Lewis

"For I know the plans I have for you," says the LORD. "They are plans for good and not for disaster, to give you a future and a hope. In those days when you pray, I will listen. If you look for me wholeheartedly, you will find me."
—Jeremiah 29:11-13 NLT

Journal Your Way to Hope

Activate God's plans by praying and seeking God wholeheartedly. When you find God, you will find His plans. As you keep on asking you purify your motives and prepare your heart to receive good gifts. When you see God as a Holy parent and giver of good gifts, your heart will surge with hope.

God has plans for you. He doesn't call you to be His child without a specific purpose. God settled all of this before He created the world (Ephesians 1:4). Therefore, you're able to activate God's plans by seeking and asking.

You don't have to wait until you know exactly what God plans for you. God will teach you His will in the context of your relationship. Be open to learning what is on God's heart. Then start asking. What do you want from God?

Truth #17

God is On Your Side, Ready to Help

*Don't be afraid, for I am with you.
Don't be discouraged, for I am your God.
I will strengthen you and help you.
I will hold you up with my victorious right hand.*
—Isaiah 41:10 NLT

God is our mighty fortress, always ready to help in times of trouble. And so, we won't be afraid! Let the earth tremble and the mountains tumble into the deepest sea.
—Psalm 46:1-2 CEV

MATT PAVLIK

Faith isn't the ability to believe long and far into the misty future. It's simply taking God at His word and taking the next step.
—Joni Erickson Tada

*Even though I walk through
the valley of the shadow of death,
I will fear no evil,
for you are with me;
your rod and your staff,
they comfort me.*
—Psalm 23:4 ESV

Journal Your Way to Hope

God is with you in high and low times. Even when you are in the midst of the lowest or scariest times of life, you need not fear. Jesus's death was not the end of Him.

Even though your circumstances may bring you down for the moment, you will rise again. You can't make life go exactly how you want it to go. But with each passing day, you can grow more secure. You can find peace and contentment from knowing God more.

Because the kingdom of God lasts forever and it's within you, you will last forever. Life's low points don't look as scary when viewed with heaven in mind. Nothing can prevent God from fulfilling His purposes for you. Ask God to reveal more of Himself so you can better understand His purpose for you.

God is With You Wherever You Go

"Have I not commanded you? Be strong and courageous. Do not be frightened, and do not be dismayed, for the LORD your God is with you wherever you go."
—Joshua 1:9 ESV

Let your character [your moral essence, your inner nature] be free from the love of money [shun greed—be financially ethical], being content with what you have; for He has said, "I WILL NEVER [under any circumstances] DESERT YOU [nor give you up nor leave you without support, nor will I in any degree leave you helpless], NOR WILL I FORSAKE or LET YOU DOWN or RELAX MY HOLD ON YOU [assuredly not]!"
—Hebrews 13:5 AMP

MATT PAVLIK

Never forget that you are not trusting to blind chance; you are trusting the God who longs to be with you.
—Pete Wilson, What Keeps You Up at Night?

Command those who are rich in this present world not to be arrogant nor to put their hope in wealth, which is so uncertain, but to put their hope in God, who richly provides us with everything for our enjoyment.
—1 Timothy 6:17 NIV

Journal Your Way to Hope

God doesn't promise to eliminate all of your suffering, instead, He promises you will never suffer alone.

God takes care of you. You don't need to worry about food, money, or other provision to fulfill God's plans. God knows what you need; He doesn't forget about you. His Spirit lives with you and knows exactly what is happening to you (Matthew 6:25-34).

Regardless of how unfulfilled you feel at any given moment, God remains steadfastly committed to your good. It's natural to feel disappointed when what you want to enjoy and what God provides may be two different things—but the truth stands: God provides extravagantly for your enjoyment. Are you hoping in God? How has He provided for you?

Truth #19

Your Suffering Assures You of Your Salvation

Therefore, since we have been made right in God's sight by faith, we have peace with God because of what Jesus Christ our Lord has done for us. Because of our faith, Christ has brought us into this place of undeserved privilege where we now stand, and we confidently and joyfully look forward to sharing God's glory. We can rejoice, too, when we run into problems and trials, for we know that they help us develop endurance. And endurance develops strength of character, and character strengthens our confident hope of salvation. And this hope will not lead to disappointment. For we know how dearly God loves us, because he has given us the Holy Spirit to fill our hearts with his love.

—Romans 5:1-5 NLT

Character cannot be developed in ease and quiet. Only through experience of trial and suffering can the soul be strengthened, ambition inspired, and success achieved. All the world is full of suffering. It is also full of overcoming.
—Helen Keller

You see, every child of God overcomes the world, for our faith is the victorious power that triumphs over the world. So who are the world conquerors, defeating its power? Those who believe that Jesus is the Son of God.
—1 John 5:4-5 TPT

Journal Your Way to Hope

Have problems been piling up around you? Ask God to help you endure. Then be sure to ask Him how to use the problems to climb higher. God is an expert overcomer. He can take the worst failures and turn them into a glorious victory.

No one wants a difficult life. No one wants to struggle. That isn't the way life is supposed to be. You might say it isn't fair. But eternity in heaven in exchange for short-term pain is a good trade. Life might not always be fun, but there's always hope and that makes it more than fair.

You are an overcoming world-conqueror. As you see the reality of God's true work in your life, you naturally become more confident. What part of God's overcoming mission has He given to you? If you don't know, ask Him for one.

Truth #20

God's Plans for Your Good Outlast Your Suffering

Praise God, the Father of our Lord Jesus Christ. God is so good, and by raising Jesus from death, he has given us new life and a hope that lives on. God has something stored up for you in heaven, where it will never decay or be ruined or disappear. You have faith in God, whose power will protect you until the last day. Then he will save you, just as he has always planned to do. On that day you will be glad, even if you have to go through many hard trials for a while.

—1 Peter 1:3-6 CEV

His Spirit lets us know that together with Christ we will be given what God has promised. We will also share in the glory of Christ, because we have suffered with him.

—Romans 8:17 CEV

MATT PAVLIK

The readiest way to escape from our sufferings is to be willing they should endure as long as God pleases.
—John Wesley

The cross means there is no shipwreck without hope; there is no dark without dawn; nor storm without haven.
—Pope John Paul II

Now all glory to God, who is able to keep you from falling away and will bring you with great joy into his glorious presence without a single fault.
—Jude 1:24 NLT

Journal Your Way to Hope

No matter how behind, backward, sinful, incomplete, or hopeless you are today, God has a plan to perfect you for His enjoyment into eternity. He has an inheritance waiting for you in heaven.

Present-day problems are always temporary. God always has a plan beyond the problems you are facing. God's power preserves you until He finally completes His act to save you. This doesn't make suffering go away, but it does make your suffering meaningful.

The more you know you have a happy, rewarding ending, the more you can endure. God is personally guaranteeing you will endure to the end because you remain in Him like a branch remains in the vine.

Truth #21

You Share in Suffering So You Can Share in Glory

Therefore we do not become discouraged [spiritless, disappointed, or afraid]. Though our outer self is [progressively] wasting away, yet our inner self is being [progressively] renewed day by day. For our momentary, light distress [this passing trouble] is producing for us an eternal weight of glory [a fullness] beyond all measure [surpassing all comparisons, a transcendent splendor and an endless blessedness]! So we look not at the things which are seen, but at the things which are unseen; for the things which are visible are temporal [just brief and fleeting], but the things which are invisible are everlasting and imperishable.

—2 Corinthians 4:16-18 AMP

MATT PAVLIK

*We must accept finite disappointment,
but never lose infinite hope.*
—Martin Luther King, Jr.

*Yet what we suffer now is nothing compared
to the glory he will reveal to us later.*
—Romans 8:18 NLT

Journal Your Way to Hope

Old-age can be a blessing when you focus on the life-wisdom you've gained. But it can also be discouraging when you focus on your body that is slowly wearing out and dying.

Your body will return to dust, but your spirit is invisible, everlasting, and imperishable. After you die, you will be clothed with a new imperishable body (1 Corinthians 15:42). Your suffering today doesn't compare to your future glory.

You might not be able to see God's love, but somehow you can know His love that surpasses understanding. What is waiting is beyond what you can imagine, but somehow your spiritual eyes can see it. So when you think you can't see, try looking with your spiritual eyes and you will find Him (Ephesians 3:19-20, 2 Corinthians 2:9-12).

Truth #22

Your Suffering and Hard Work Are Not in Vain

This is why we work hard and continue to struggle, for our hope is in the living God, who is the Savior of all people and particularly of all believers.
—1 Timothy 4:10 NLT

Trust in the Lord with all your heart; do not depend on your own understanding. Seek his will in all you do and he will show you which path to take.
—Proverbs 3:5-6 NLT

Journal Your Way to Hope

Old-age can be a blessing when you focus on the life-wisdom you've gained. But it can also be discouraging when you focus on your body that is slowly wearing out and dying.

Your body will return to dust, but your spirit is invisible, everlasting, and imperishable. After you die, you will be clothed with a new imperishable body (1 Corinthians 15:42). Your suffering today doesn't compare to your future glory.

You might not be able to see God's love, but somehow you can know His love that surpasses understanding. What is waiting is beyond what you can imagine, but somehow your spiritual eyes can see it. So when you think you can't see, try looking with your spiritual eyes and you will find Him (Ephesians 3:19-20, 2 Corinthians 2:9-12).

Truth #22

Your Suffering and Hard Work Are Not in Vain

This is why we work hard and continue to struggle, for our hope is in the living God, who is the Savior of all people and particularly of all believers.
—1 Timothy 4:10 NLT

Trust in the Lord with all your heart; do not depend on your own understanding. Seek his will in all you do and he will show you which path to take.
—Proverbs 3:5-6 NLT

MATT PAVLIK

You take the negative, the bitter, the pain, the suffering, the depression, and all of those are ingredients for something far more purposeful than you can imagine.

—Lecrae

Beloved, do not be surprised at the fiery trial when it comes upon you to test you, as though something strange were happening to you. But rejoice insofar as you share Christ's sufferings, that you may also rejoice and be glad when his glory is revealed.

—1 Peter 4:12-13 ESV

Journal Your Way to Hope

God's promises are real, so your hard work is not in vain. Your life is not a waste. Your existence is not pointless. How do I know this? God created you as a custom instrument; the melody He can make through you will create a symphony never heard before as you accomplish His purposes.

Because of suffering, life can seem like a bad dream. You long to wake up and be done with suffering. But God has you here for a reason (2 Corinthians 5:6-10, Philippians 1:20-24).

Your suffering may not make sense to you. God's promises may seem like they will never come true. But if you don't suffer in this life, something must be wrong. Real hope focuses on God beyond the suffering. What is it like to wake up from a bad dream into a glorious new reality?

God Satisfies Your Soul

*For he satisfies the longing soul,
and the hungry soul he fills with good things.*
—Psalm 107:9 ESV

And this same God who takes care of me will supply all your needs from his glorious riches, which have been given to us in Christ Jesus.
—Philippians 4:19 NLT

MATT PAVLIK

*God often gives in one brief moment that
which He has for a long time denied.*
—Thomas a Kempis

*"The LORD is my portion," says my soul,
"therefore I will hope in him."
The LORD is good to those who wait for him,
to the soul who seeks him.*
—Lamentations 3:24-25 NLT

Journal Your Way to Hope

Biblical waiting means seeking God. Seek God when you feel empty or directionless. You'll never be disappointed when you seek God. God is capable of satisfying your soul like no other thing. When God serves up a portion of Himself, you can eat from an abundance and overflow.

God is preparing you for more enjoyment and responsibility. He doesn't take short-cuts; He is building you to last forever. This requires patient endurance while He makes you ready. Purifying your motives takes time. Growing is hard work.

God has important work and amazing blessings for you. God will grant you your heart's desire (Psalm 37:4, Luke 19:11-27). Where is God showing persistence in nourishing your soul? What do you imagine God is preparing to give you?

Truth #24

God Fills You
With Joy, Peace, and Hope

I give you peace, the kind of peace that only I can give. It isn't like the peace that this world can give. So don't be worried or afraid.

—John 4:27 CEV

May the God of hope fill you with all joy and peace in believing, so that by the power of the Holy Spirit you may abound in hope.

—Romans 15:13 ESV

MATT PAVLIK

Hope is to our spirits what oxygen is to our lungs. Lose hope and you die. They may not bury you for awhile, but without hope you are dead inside. The only way to face the future is to fly straight into it on the wings of hope.... hope is the energy of the soul. Hope is the power of tomorrow.

—Lewis B. Smedes

Now may our Lord Jesus Christ himself and God our Father, who loved us and by his grace gave us eternal comfort and a wonderful hope, comfort you and strengthen you in every good thing you do and say.

—2 Thessalonians 2:16-17 NLT

Journal Your Way to Hope

When all else fails, cling to your belief in God's goodness because it will produce joy and peace which results in hope.

Are you ready to fly into the future? Being able to hope might sound too good to be true. That's the point. There is more to come than platitudes. Believing God's promises is the key to abounding in hope, joy, and peace. The result of your belief should be joy, peace, and faith put into action. When you're anxious, you can lose focus on what you believe.

Jesus says it only takes faith the size of a mustard seed to accomplish something great (Luke 17:6). How can this be? Faith is potent stuff. It's pure. It's super-concentrated. Do you believe there is more? Take some time to imagine what good things will be coming into your life.

God is an Endless Supply of Strength

*Do you not know?
Have you not heard?
The LORD is the everlasting God,
the Creator of the ends of the earth.
He will not grow tired or weary,
and his understanding no one can fathom.
He gives strength to the weary
and increases the power of the weak.
Even youths grow tired and weary,
and young men stumble and fall;
but those who hope in the LORD
will renew their strength.
They will soar on wings like eagles;
they will run and not grow weary,
they will walk and not be faint.*

—Isaiah 40:28-31 NIV

MATT PAVLIK

While the resurrection promises us a new and perfect life in the future, God loves us too much to leave us alone to contend with the pain, guilt and loneliness of our present life.

—Josh McDowell

*The Lord is my strength,
the reason for my song,
because he has saved me.
I praise and honor the Lord—
he is my God and
the God of my ancestors.*

—Exodus 15:2 CEV

Journal Your Way to Hope

When you hope in God's grace, God's Spirit moves within you. You have the power to be free and bold. You can act with strength and confidence.

If your hope is genuine, your actions might seem faithful to you but careless to others. You are free to exercise your faith to accomplish the irrational and exceptional. You can pass on worldly short-term gain and instead invest long-term with all that God has provided.

Pray for God's strength: *God, increase my hope and trust in You. I want to experience You actively transforming me into Your image. Your grace grants me freedom, boldness, and needed transformation. I hope in Your grace so that I can be prepared for bold action.*

Journal Your Way to Hope

Hoping in the Lord is an active, conscious process. Recognizing that God is both present with you and sustaining you will renew your strength. God doesn't run low on strength. While God doesn't eliminate the difficulty, He will do what is necessary to strengthen you.

Hope brings strength. Hope revives your spirit. When you find hope, you find the resolve to endure anything. But even then, whatever God allows in your life isn't random—it always serves His purposes (Ephesians 1:11).

God is a winner. His plans make you a winner, too. Jesus suffered and died before God resurrected Him. Life can appear hopeless, but God has deeper plans and purposes that the enemy can't touch. God's reserves are endless.

Truth #26

Confident Hope
Leads to Bold Action

Therefore, since we have such a hope, we are very bold. Now the Lord is the Spirit, and where the Spirit of the Lord is, there is freedom. And we all, who with unveiled faces contemplate the Lord's glory, are being transformed into his image with ever-increasing glory, which comes from the Lord, who is the Spirit.

—2 Corinthians 3:12, 17, 18 NIV

And everyone who has given up houses or brothers or sisters or father or mother or children or property, for my sake, will receive a hundred times as much in return and will inherit eternal life.

—Matthew 19:29 NLT

MATT PAVLIK

Everything that is done in this world is done by hope.
—Martin Luther

Therefore, preparing your minds for action, and being sober-minded, set your hope fully on the grace that will be brought to you at the revelation of Jesus Christ.
—1 Peter 1:13 ESV

Truth #27

God's Will is That You Become Complete

And I am sure of this, that he who began a good work in you will bring it to completion at the day of Jesus Christ.
—Philippians 1:6 ESV

Now may the God of peace himself sanctify you completely, and may your whole spirit and soul and body be kept blameless at the coming of our Lord Jesus Christ. He who calls you is faithful; he will surely do it.
—1 Thessalonians 5:23-24 ESV

MATT PAVLIK

God does not give us everything we want, but He does fulfill His promises, leading us along the best and straightest paths to Himself.
—Dietrich Bonhoeffer

Yes, I am the vine; you are the branches. Those who remain in me, and I in them, will produce much fruit. For apart from me you can do nothing. But if you remain in me and my words remain in you, you may ask for anything you want, and it will be granted!
—John 15:5,7 NLT

Journal Your Way to Hope

You're a work in progress. God wants you to grow up and be capable of acting more like Him. As you live connected to God, both your growth and your completion in God's image are inevitable. It's natural to want God to make life easier. But God won't let anything get in the way of your growth. He wants to complete His eternally significant work in you.

As you seek and prioritize God's kingdom, you're able to realize how much some parts of life are non-essential. Here are some prayers God always eagerly answers:
- Make me more like Jesus.
- Help me bear more fruit.
- Show me who you are.
- Wash me clean from my sin.
- Love me, so I know how to love others.

Truth #28

God Strengthens You to Endure All Things

I can do all things through him who strengthens me.
—Philippians 4:13 ESV

We also pray that you will be strengthened with all his glorious power so you will have all the endurance and patience you need. May you be filled with joy, always thanking the Father. He has enabled you to share in the inheritance that belongs to his people, who live in the light. For he has rescued us from the kingdom of darkness and transferred us into the Kingdom of his dear Son, who purchased our freedom and forgave our sins.
—Colossians 1:11-14 NLT

MATT PAVLIK

Perseverance is more than endurance. It is endurance combined with absolute assurance and certainty that what we are looking for is going to happen.
—Oswald Chambers

We give great honor to those who endure under suffering. For instance, you know about Job, a man of great endurance. You can see how the Lord was kind to him at the end, for the Lord is full of tenderness and mercy.
—James 5:11 NLT

Journal Your Way to Hope

Like Paul, you can endure all kinds of situations because God is constantly strengthening you. Remain in the vine (Jesus) to continue to receive strength. Worldly endurance is based on white-knuckled will-power. But you have a connection to God which brings hope, power, and strength which allow you to persevere.

Perseverance is endurance plus hope. You persevere for a reward. If there is only pain without reward, you endure for nothing (1 Corinthians 15:19). The person without God hopes (without assurance) that the after-life may offer something better. The reward you work for isn't to gain entrance into heaven. You work to build God's kingdom as a co-heir with Christ (Romans 8:17). Your inheritance is guaranteed.

Truth #29

God Doesn't Want You To Give Up or Lose Hope

Here's what I've learned through it all: Don't give up; don't be impatient; be entwined as one with the Lord. Be brave and courageous, and never lose hope. Yes, keep on waiting—for he will never disappoint you!

—Psalm 27:14 TPT

Let this hope burst forth within you, releasing a continual joy. Don't give up in a time of trouble, but commune with God at all times.

—Romans 12:12 TPT

MATT PAVLIK

*Be sure you put your feet in the right place,
then stand firm.*
—Abraham Lincoln

*One day Jesus taught the apostles to keep praying
and never stop or lose hope.*
—Luke 18:1 TPT

Journal Your Way to Hope

Where are you standing? Don't give up even when all else fails. The world looks at the waiting Christian and laughs; God desires that you experience the power of His kingdom, finish strong, and receive the prize He has waiting for you.

God has never failed to show up—meaning—His plans always reach fulfillment. Your dreams might have already died, but God can resurrect them (John 11:1-44). Your trust pleases God and when God finally acts, blessings are sure to follow (Hebrews 11:6).

God wants you to pray and ask for what you need. Asking is never a burden to Him. Strengthen your hope and belief by meditating on God's promises. What is God promising you now? In the future? For eternity?

Truth #30

When God Gave You Life, He Gave You Dreams

When hope's dream seems to drag on and on, the delay can be depressing. But when at last your dream comes true, life's sweetness will satisfy your soul.
—Proverbs 13:12 TPT

Commit your actions to the LORD, and your plans will succeed.
—Proverbs 16:3 NLT

MATT PAVLIK

If you lose hope, somehow you lose the vitality that keeps moving, you lose that courage to be, that quality that helps you go on in spite of it all. And so today I still have a dream.
—Martin Luther King Jr

*We make our own plans,
but the Lord decides
where we will go.*

*We make our own decisions,
but the Lord alone determines what happens.*
—Proverbs 16:9, 33 CEV

Journal Your Way to Hope

Pursuing your dreams isn't much different than learning how to walk. If you stumble badly, you won't be overwhelmed because God holds your hand (Psalm 37:24). God is in control.

God is working to cause His purposes to be fulfilled even when you don't know what to do. Genuine hope will sustain you when you encounter delays and suffering. Rest peacefully because God has the ability to direct your steps and make the most of them.

All dreams start as a seed that God planted in you. After you commit your ways to the Lord, dare to risk, dare to dream. Trust the seeds that God planted within you. Keep watering and fertilizing them. What dream is God calling you to courageously launch, trusting in Him to reach your goal?

JOURNAL IN LAYERS

Did you complete the first pass through these truths? Remember to revisit the truths and your writing to gain the full benefit. You might be amazed at what you understood at first. But you can learn more with each pass you make.

To gain the most from journaling, here are some other journal-in-layers techniques to try:
- Return at a regular interval to followup with your previous entry. This is the secret to developing deeper truth in your heart.
- Limit the number of truths you explore in each layer. For example, focus on the first seven truths in a week. Revisit them each week for four weeks. Or, if God is speaking to you through one particular truth, focus on it for several days.
- Focus on only one scripture at a time. Review one verse from each lesson, then journal another layer.
- Focus on the lesson's quote or picture.
- Draw your own picture that represents the truth.
- Write your own prayer in response to the lesson.
- Focus on one particular emotion you feel as you read the lesson. Write about that feeling and other times you've felt that way.
- Focus on the past if you need healing. Focus on the present if you feel anxious. Focus on the future if you feel restless.

Have you tried another technique that works for you? Would you like to share how has this book been a blessing to you? Contact me at mpavlik@christianconcepts.com. You can learn more about journaling by getting *Soar Like Eagles* at ChristianConcepts.com.

ABOUT MATT PAVLIK

Matt Pavlik is a licensed professional clinical counselor who wants each individual restored to their true identity. He completed his Masters in Clinical Pastoral Counseling from Ashland Theological Seminary and his Bachelors in Computer Science from the University of Illinois.

He's been a Christian since 1991 and started journaling around that time. Matt and his wife Georgette have been married since 1999 and live with their four children in Centerville, Ohio.

Blogger

Learn more at ChristianConcepts.com.

Professional Counselor

Matt has more than 15 years of experience counseling individuals and couples at his Christian private practice, New Reflections Counseling (NewReflectionsCounseling.com).

Author

In addition to *To Identity and Beyond* (see ToIdentityAndBeyond.com), he has authored two workbooks: one on identity and the other on marriage (see ConfidentIdentity.com and MarriageFromRootsToFruits.com).

Coming Soon

If you like *Journal Your Way To Hope*, you'll love these other titles:
- *Journal Your Way To Significance*
- *Journal Your Way To Love*
- *Journal Your Way To Security*

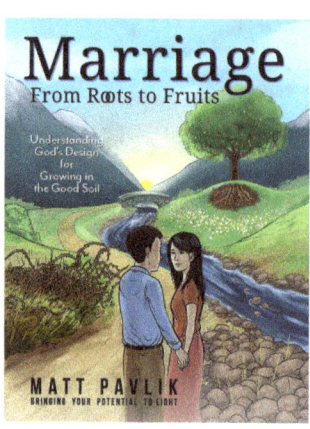